Athena Gardner

The Alexandrian and Gardnerian Book of Shadows

Authors Choice Press

San Jose   New York   Lincoln   Shanghai

Authors Choice Press
an imprint of iUniverse.com, Inc.

For information address:
iUniverse.com, Inc.
620 North 48th Street, Suite 201
Lincoln, NE 68504-3467
www.iuniverse.com

Originally published by Star Rising

ISBN: 0-595-12845-9

Printed in the United States of America

Contents

Preface

This is the original text of the Alexandrian Book of Shadows. This has exceptional ceremonies for the adept. Please study Wicca thoroughly before attempting any rituals or magic. It is not something to take lightly and trying magic before you are ready can cause you to learn a lot before you need to. You can learn the hard way or the easy way.

This book is dedicated to the One Source and is intended to bring forth knowledge and light to those seeking this knowledge. Please, if you are seeking to harm someone through magic or are considering it for selfish gain you might want to look elsewhere. Magic without knowledge can have a severe impact on ones life, and I mean the inexperienced person performing the magic on another. All things return seven fold.

To you this knowledge is given.

Blessed Be!

The Laws

THE OLD LAW

1.The Law was made and ordained of old.

2.The Law was made for the Wicca, to advise and help in their troubles.

3.The Wicca should give due worship to the gods and obey their will, which they ordain, for it was made for the good of Wicca as the worship of the Wicca is good for the gods. For the gods love the brethren of Wicca.

4.As a man loveth a woman by mastering her,

5.So should the Wicca love the gods by being mastered by them.

6.And it is necessary that the Circle which is the temple of the gods, should be truly cast and purified. And that it may be a fit place for the gods to enter.

7.And the Wicca shall be properly prepared and purified to enter into the presence of the gods.

8.With love and worship in their hearts, they shall raise power from their bodies to give power to the gods.

9.As has been taught of old.

10.For in this way only may men have communion with the gods, for the gods cannot help man without the help of man.

HPS & HP

11.And the High Priestess shall rule her coven as the representative of the Goddess.

12.And the High Priest shall support her as the representative of the God.

13.And the High Priestess shall choose whom she will, be he of sufficient rank, to be her High Priest.

14.For, as the God Himself kissed Her feet in the five-fold salute, laying His power at the feet of the Goddess because of Her youth and beauty, Her sweetness and kindness, Her wisdom and justice, Her humility and generosity,

15.So He resigned all His power to Her.

16.But the High Priestess should ever mind that the power comes from Him.

17.It is only lent, to be used wisely and justly.

18.And the greatest virtue of a High Priestess be that she recognize that youth is necessary to the representative of the Goddess.

19.So she will gracefully retire in favour of a younger woman should the Coven so decide in council.

20.For a true High Priestess realizes that gracefully surrendering pride of place is one of the greatest virtues.

21.And that thereby she will return to that pride of place in another life, with greater power and beauty.

SECURITY

22.In the old days, when witchdom extended far, we were free and worshipped in all the greater temples.

23.But in these unhappy times we must celebrate our sacred mysteries in secret.

24.So be it ordained that none but the Wicca may see our mysteries, for our enemies are many and torture loosens the tongue of man.

25.So be it ordained that no Coven shall know where the next Coven bide.

26.Or who its members be, save only the Priest and Priestess and messenger.

27.And there shall be no communication between them, save by the messenger of the gods, or the summoner.

28.And only if it be safe may the Covens meet in some safe place for the great festivals.

29.And while there, none shall say whence they came nor give their true names.

30.To this end, that if any be tortured, in their agony, they may not tell if they do not know.

31.So be it ordained that no one shall tell anyone not of the craft who be of the Wicca, nor give any names or where they bide, or in any way tell anything which can betray any of us to our foes.

32.Nor may he tell where the Covendom be.

33.Or the Covenstead.

34.Or where the meetings be.

35.And if any break these Laws, even under torture, **THE CURSE OF THE GODDESS SHALL BE UPON THEM**, so they may never be reborn on earth and may remain where they belong, in the hell of the Christians.

DISPUTES

36.Let each High Priestess govern her Coven with justice and love, with the help and advice of the High Priest and the Elders, always heeding the advice of the Messenger of the Gods if he cometh.

37.She will heed all complaints of all Brothers and strive to settle all differences among them.

38.But it must be recognized that there will always be people who will ever strive to force others to do as they will.

39.These are not necessarily evil.

40.And they oft have good ideas and such ideas should be talked over in council.

41.But if they will not agree with their Brothers, or if they say,

42."I will not work under this High Priestess,"

43.It hath ever been the Old Law to be convenient to the Brethren and to avoid disputes.

NEW COVENS

44.Any of the third may claim to found a new Coven because they live over a league away from the Covenstead or are about to do so.

45.Anyone living within the Covendom and wishing to form a new Coven, shall tell the Elders of their intention, and on the instant avoid their dwelling and remove to the new Covendom.

46.Members of the old Coven may join the new one when it is formed. But if they do, they must utterly avoid the old Coven.

47.The Elders of the new and old Covens should meet in peace and brotherly love to decide the new boundaries.

48.Those of the craft who dwell outside both Covendoms may join either but not both.

49.Though all may, if the Elders agree, meet for the great festivals if it be truly in peace and brotherly love,

50.But splitting the Coven oft means strife, so for this reason these Laws were made of old and may the **CURSE OF THE GODDESS BE ON ANY WHO DISREGARD THEM**. So be it ordained.

GRIMOIRE

51.If you would keep a book, let it be in your own hand of write. Let brothers and sisters copy what they will, but never let the book out of your hands, and never keep the writings of another.

52.For if it be found in their hand of write, they may be taken and arraigned.

53.Let each guard his own writings and destroy them whenever danger threatens.

54.Learn as much as you may by heart and, when danger is past, rewrite your book, an it be safe.

55.For this reason, if any die, destroy their book an they have not been able to.

56.For, an it be found, 'tis clear proof against them.

57.And our oppressors know well "Ye may not be a witch alone".

58.So all their kin and friends be in danger of torture,

59.So destroy everything not necessary.

60.If your book be found on you, 'tis clear proof against you alone, you may be arraigned.

PERSECUTION

61.Keep all thoughts of the craft from your mind.

62.If the torture be too great to bear, say "I will confess. I cannot bear this torture. What do you want me to say?"

63.If they try to make you speak of the Brotherhood, do not.

64.But if they try to make you speak of impossibilities such as flying through the air, consorting with a Christian devil or sacrificing children, or eating men's flesh,

65.To obtain relief from torture say "I had an evil dream, I was beside myself, I was crazed."

66.Not all magistrates are bad, if there be an excuse, they may show mercy.

67.If you have confessed aught, deny it afterwards, say you babbled under torture, say you knew not what you said.

68.If you are condemned, fear not.

69.The Brotherhood is powerful and will help you to escape if you stand steadfast, but if you betray aught there is no hope for you in this life or in that to come.

70.Be sure, if steadfast you go to the pyre, drugs will reach you, you will feel naught. You go to death and what lies beyond, the ecstasy of the goddess.

TOOLS

71.To avoid discovery, let the working tools be as ordinary things that any may have in their houses.

72.Let the pentacles be of wax so that they may be broken at once or melted.

73.Have no sword unless your rank allows it.

74.Have no names or signs on anything.

75.Write the names and signs on them in ink before consecrating them and wash it off immediately afterwards.

76.Let the colours of the hilts tell which is which.

77.Do not engrave them lest they cause discovery.

CONDUCT

78.Ever remember ye are the hidden children of the Goddess so never do anything to disgrace them or Her.

79.Never boast, never threaten, never say you would wish ill of any-one.

80.If any person not in the Circle, speak of the craft, say, "Speak not to me of such, it frightens me, 'tis evil luck to speak of it."

81.For this reason, the Christians have their spies everywhere. These speak as if they were well affected to us, as if they would come to our meetings, saying, "My mother used to worship the Old Ones. I would I could go myself."

82.To such as these, ever deny all knowledge.

83.But to others, ever say, "'Tis foolish men talk of witches flying through the air. To do so they must be as light as thistledown. And men say that witches all be blear-eyed old crones, so what pleasure can there be at a witch meeting such as folks talk on ?"

84.And say, "Many wise men now say there be no such creatures."

85.Ever make it jest) and in some future time perhaps, the persecu-tion may die and we may worship our gods in safety again.

86.Let us all pray for that happy day.

87.May the blessings of the Goddess and God be on all who keep these Laws which are ordained.

VALUABLES

88.If the craft hath any appanage, let all guard it and help to keep it clear and good for the craft.

89.And let all justly guard all monies of the craft.

90.And if any Brother truly wrought it, 'tis right they have their pay, an it be just. An this be not taking money for the art, but for good and honest work.

91.And even the Christians say, "The labourer is worthy of his hire," but if any Brother work willingly for the good of the craft without pay, 'tis but to their greater honour. So be it ordained.

QUARRELS

92.If there be any dispute or quarrel among the Brethren, the High Priestess shall straightly convene the Elders and inquire into the matter, and they shall hear both sides, first alone and then together.

93.And they shall decide justly, not favouring one side or the other.

94.Ever recognising there be people who can never agree to work under others.

95.But at the same time, there be some people who cannot rule justly.

96.To those who must ever be chief, there is one answer.

97."'Void the Coven or seek another one, or make a Coven of your own, taking with you those who will go."

98.To those who cannot rule justly, the answer be, "Those who cannot bear your rule will leave you."

99.For none may come to meetings with those with whom they are at variance.

100.So, an either cannot agree, get hence, for the craft must ever survive. So be it ordained.

CURSES

101.   In the olden days when we had power, we could use the art

against any who ill-treated the Brotherhood. But in these evil days we must not do so. For our enemies have devised a burning pit of everlasting fire into which they say their god casteth all the people who worship him, except it be the very few who are released by their priest's spells and masses. And this be chiefly by giving monies and rich gifts to receive his favour for their great god is ever in need of money.

102. But as our gods need our aid to make fertility for man and crops, so is the god of the Christians ever in need of man's help to search out and destroy us. Their priests ever tell them that any who get our help are damned to this hell forever, so men be mad with the terror of it.

103. But they make men believe that they may escape this hell if they give victims to the tormentors. So for this reason all be forever spying, thinking, "An I can catch but one of these Wicca, I will escape from this fiery pit."

104. So for this reason we have our hidels, and men searching long and not finding, say, "There be none, or if there be, they be in a far country."

105. But when one of our oppressors die, or even be sick, ever is the cry, "This be witches' malice", and the hunt is up again. And though they slay ten of their own to one of ours, still they care not. They have countless thousands.

106. While we are few indeed. So be it ordained.

107. That none shall use the art in any way to do ill to any.

108. However much they may injure us, harm none. And nowtimes many believe we exist not.

109. That this Law shall ever continue to help us in our plight, no one, however great an injury or injustice they receive, may use the

art in any way to do ill, or harm any. But they may, after great consultations with all, use the art to restrain Christians from harming us Brothers, but only to constrain them and never to punish.

110. To this end men will say, "Such a one is a mighty searcher out, and a persecutor of old women whom they deemeth to be witches, and none hath done him harm, so it be proof that they cannot or more truly there be none."

111. For all know full well that so many folk have died because someone had a grudge against them, or were persecuted because they had money or goods to sieze, or because they had none to bribe the searchers. And many have died because they were scolding old women. So much that men now say that only old women are witches.

112. And this be to our advantage and turns suspicion away from us.

113. In England and Scotland 'tis now many a year since a witch hath died the death. But any misuse of the power might raise the persecution again.

114. So never break this Law, however much you are tempted, and never consent to its being broken in the least.

115. If you know it is being broken, you must work strongly against it.

116. And any High Priestess or High Priest who consents to its breach must immediately be deposed for 'tis the blood of the Brethren they endanger.

117. Do good, an it be safe, and only if it be safe.

118. And keep strictly to the Old Law.

PAYMENT

119. Never accept money for the use of the art, for money ever smeareth the taker. 'Tis sorcerors and conjurers and the priests of the Christians who ever accept money for the use of their arts. And they sell pardons to let men ascape from their sins.

120. Be not as these. If you accept no money, you will be free from temptation to use the art for evil causes.

121. All may use the art for their own advantage or for the advantage of the craft only if you are sure you harm none.

122. But ever let the Coven debate this at length. Only if all are satisfied that none may be harmed, may the art be used.

123. If it is not possible to achieve your ends one way, perchance the aim may be achieved by acting in a different way so as to harm none. **MAY THE CURSE OF THE GODDESS BE ON ANY WHO BREAKETH THIS LAW**. So be it ordained.

124. 'Tis judged lawful if ever any of the craft need a house or land and none will sell, to incline the owner's mind so as to be willing to sell, provided it harmeth him not in any way and the full price is paid without haggling.

125. Never bargain or cheapen anything whilst you buy by the art. So be it ordained.

LAW OF THE LAND

126. "Tis the Old Law and the most important of all laws, that no one may do anything which will endanger any of the craft, or bring them into contact with the law of the land or any persecutors.

127. In any dispute between Brethren, no one may invoke any laws

but those of the craft.

128. Or any tribunal but that of the Priestess, Priest and Elders.

DISCUSSION OF WITCHCRAFT

129. It is not forbidden to say as Christians do, "There be witchcraft in the land," because our oppressors of old make it a heresy not to believe in witchcraft and so a crime to deny it which thereby puts you under suspicion.

130. But ever say, "I know not of it here, perchance there may be but afar off, I know not where."

131. But ever speak of them as old crones, consorting with the devil and riding through the air.

132. And ever say, "But how may many ride the air if they be not as light as thistledown."

133. But the curse of the Goddess be on any who cast suspicion on any of the Brotherhood.

134. Or who speak of any real meeting-place or where they bide.

WORTCUNNING

135. the craft keep books with the names of all herbs which are good, and all cures so all may learn.

136. But keep another book with all the Bales and Apies and let only the Elders and other trustworthy people have this knowledge. So be it ordained.

137. And may the blessings of the gods be on all who keep these Laws, and the curses of both the God and the Goddess be on all who

break them.

USE OF THE ART

138. Remember the art is the secret of the gods and may only be used in earnest and never for show or vainglory.

139. Magicians and Christians may taunt us saying, "You have no power, show us your power. Do magic before our eyes, then only will we believe," seeking to cause us to betray the art before them.

140. Heed them not, for the art is holy and may only be used in need, and the curse of the gods be on any who break this Law.

RESIGNATIONS

141. It ever be the way with women and with men also, that they ever seek new love.

142. Nor should we reprove them for this.

143. But it may be found a disadvantage to the craft.

144. And so many a time it has happened that a High Priest or a High Priestess, impelled by love, hath departed with their love. That is, they left the Coven.

145. Now if the High Priestess wishes to resign, she may do so in full Coven.

146. And this resignation is valid.

147. But if they should run off without resigning, who may know if they may not return in a few months?

148. So the Law is, if a High Priestess leaves her Coven, she be taken

back and all be as before.

149. Meanwhile, if she has a deputy, that deputy shall act as High Priestess for as long as the High Priestess is away.

150. If she returns not at the end of a year and a day, then shall the Coven elect a new High Priestess,

151. Unless there is a good reason to the contrary.

152. The person who has done the work should reap the benefit of the reward. If somebody else is elected, the deputy is made maiden and deputy of the High Priestess.

TRAINING

153. It has been found that practicing the art doth cause a fondness between aspirant and tutor, and it is the cause of better results if this be so.

154. And if for any reason this be undesireable, it can easily be avoided by both persons from the outset firmly resolving in their minds to be as brother and sister or parent and child.

155. And it is for this reason that a man may be taught only by a woman and a woman by a man, and women and women should not attempt these practices together. So be it ordained.

PUNISHMENT

156. Order and discipline must be kept.

157. A High Priestess or a High Priest may, and should, punish all faults.

158. To this end all the craft must receive correction willingly.

159. All properly prepared, the culprit kneeling should be told his fault and his sentence pronounced.

160. Punishment should be followed by something amusing.

161. The culprit must acknowledge the justice of the punishment by kissing the hand on receiving sentence and again thanking for punishment received. So be it ordained.

Athena Gardner

The Wiccan Redes

Bide the Wiccan Redes ye must,
    In Perfect Love and Perfect Trust;
Live ye must and let to live,
    Fairly take and fairly give;
Form the Circle thrice about,
    To keep unwelcome spirits out;
Bind fast the spell every time,
    Let the words be spoke in rhyme.

Soft of eye and light of touch,
    Speak ye little, listen much;
Deosil go by waxing moon,
    Sing and dance the Witches' Rune;
Widdershins go by waning moon,
    Chant ye then a baleful tune;
When the Lady's moon is new,
    Kiss hand to her times two;
When the moon rides at peak,
    Heart's desire then ye seek.

Heed the North wind's mighty gale,
    Lock the door & trim the sail;
When the wind comes from the South,
    Love will kiss them on the mouth;
When the wind blows from the West,
    departed souls have no rest;
When the wind blows from the East,
    Expect the new and set the feast.

Nine woods in the cauldron go,
    Burn them quick, burn them slow;
Elder be the Lady's tree,
    Burn it not or curs'd ye'll be;
When the wind begins to turn,
    Soon Beltane fires will burn;

When the wheel has turned to Yule,
    light the log, the Horned One rules.

Heed the flower, bush or tree
    By the Lady blessed be'
When the rippling waters flow
    cast a stone - the truth you'll know;
When ye have & hold a need,
    Hearken not to others' greed;
With a fool no seasons spend,
    Or be counted as his friend.

Merry meet and merry part
    Bright the cheeks, warm the heart;
Mind the threefold law ye should,
    Three times bad and three times good;
Whene'er misfortune is enow,
    Wear the star upon your brow;
True in troth ever ye be
    Lest thy love prove false to thee.

'Tis by the sun that life be won,
    And by the moon that change be done;
If ye would clear the path to will,
    Make certain the mind be still;
What good be tools without Inner Light?
    What good be magic without wisdom-sight?
Eight words the Wiccan Rede fulfill -
    An it harm none, do what ye will.

Athena Gardner

Various Aphorisms

For witches this be Law -
Where ye enter in, from there withdraw.

An ye will secure the spell,
Cast some silver in the well.

Enhance thy trance
With drug and dance.

Vervain and dill lend aid to will.

Trefoil, vervain, St.-John's-wort, dill,
Hinder witches of their will !

Upon the clock, dependeth not.

Success pursueth the persistent.

Guilt flees when none pursueth.

Power shared is power lost.

Seek thine enemy in secret.

Thoughts are things: as a man thinkest, so he is.

No one person can accomplish all.

Danger is never overcome without danger.

The past is fixed, yet the future may be bent.

Where communication fails, confusion follows.

Some things cannot be understood by mortal man.

Many such must simply be accepted.

Rush in where angels fear to tread: the Gods are with you.

As a man thinketh, so is he.

If you think small, you become small.

Remember the Passwords: Perfect Love and Perfect Trust, so trust the Universe and be at Home everywhere.

If you imagine and fear 'I will get trapped', of course you will get trapped. Fear not, and you won't.

You are never less alone than when you think you are alone.

Fear not, for fear is failure and the forerunner of failure.

Pray to the Moon when she is round
Luck with you shall then abound
What you seek for shall be found
In sea or sky or solid ground ...

The Tenets

Reincarnation

Learning

Balance

Harmony

Love

Trust

Humility

Tolerance

Casting the Circle

Needs: Altar, 2 Altar Candles, Water Bowl, Salt Dish, Pentacle, Censer, Athame, Bell; Presence Lamp; 4 Quarter Candles; Sword (optional), Candle Snuffer (optional)
Let all be fit to enter into the presence of the Gods.
Start in the dark.
Ritual Leader waits until it feels like time to begin, then rises:

LIGHTING OF THE CANDLE:
R:
I light this Candle   *(lights Presence Lamp)*
in the name of that ancient presence,
which is, was, and ever shall be
male, female, all-knowing, all-powerful
and present everywhere.

And in the names of the four Mighty Ones,
the rulers of the elements,
may power and blessing descend
in this hour upon this place
and those gathered here.

R lights the two altar candles, the charcoal, and the four quarter candles from the Presence Lamp.

EXORCISM OF THE WATER:
R kneels before the altar and places the Water Bowl upon the Pentacle.
R purifies the water by plunging the tip of his/her athame into the water, saying:

R:
I exorcise thee, O Creature of Water, that thou cast out from thee all the impurity and uncleanliness of the world of phantasm. In the names of Cernunnos and Cerridwen.

BLESSING OF THE SALT:

R sets the Water Bowl aside and in its place sets the Salt Dish upon the Pentacle. R touches salt with tip of athame, saying:

R:

Blessings be upon thee, O Creature of Salt; let all malignity and hindrance be cast forth from thee, and let all good enter within. Wherefore do I bless and consecrate thee, that thou mayest aid me. In the names of Cernunnos and Cerridwen.

Using the tip of the athame, R takes three measures of salt and puts it into the water, then stirs deosil three times with the athame, saying:

R:

But ever mind that as water and salt purifies the body, so the scourge purifies the soul. So mote it be!

CASTING THE CIRCLE:

R draws a circle, continuous from north deosil unto north with the Sword (or athame), saying:

R:

I conjure thee, O Circle of Power, that thou beest a boundary between the world of men and the realms of the Mighty Ones; a meeting place of love and joy and truth; a shield against all wickedness and evil; a rampart and protection that shall preserve and contain the power that we raise within thee. Wherefore do I bless thee, and consecrate thee, in the names of Cernunnos and Cerridwen.

(If others are without, a gate is opened, and they are now brought into the Circle with a kiss, and the Circle is resealed.)

CONSECRATION OF THE CIRCLE WITH THE FOUR ELEMENTS:

R takes up the consecrated water and asperges the Circle with his/her fingertips, from north deosil unto north; and then touches each person within with the water, being touched in turn by his/her working partner (or another of the opposite sex to R, if available). Water Bowl is returned to altar.

R then takes up the censer, and likewise censes the Circle from north unto north.

Lastly R takes around the Presence Lamp (or a candle lit from the Presence Lamp and returned to it).

CALLING THE MIGHTY ONES:

All stand and salute the East. R stands in front of group facing East. Maiden stands at back of group with the Bell. M rings Bell. With athame, R draws three deosil circles and then an invoking earth pentagram, saying:

R:

Ye Lords of the Watchtowers of the East, ye Lords of Air; I, N....., do summon, stir and call you up, to witness our rites and guard the Circle!

All turn and face South. Ritual Leader and Maiden move to corresponding positions; others just turn in place. M rings Bell. With athame, R draws three deosil circles and then an invoking earth pentagram, saying:

R:

Ye Lords of the Watchtowers of the South, ye Lords of Fire; I, N....., do summon, stir and call you up, to witness our rites and guard the Circle!

Similarly, in West:

R:

Ye Lords of the Watchtowers of the West, ye Lords of Water; Lords of Death and Initiation; I, N....., do summon, stir and call you up, to witness our rites and guard the Circle!

And in North:

R:

Ye Lords of the Watchtowers of the North, ye Lords of Earth; Boreas, thou Guardian of the Northern Portals; I, N....., do summon, stir and call you up, to witness our rites and guard the Circle!

All turn back to the East and salute.

Now all turn to North again. M rings Bell. R says:
R:
Ye Mighty Ones,
Lords of the Watchtowers of the Universe,
Dread Lords of the outer spaces,
Thou powerful God, thou gentle Goddess,
We invite you to our meeting.
(pause)
O thou Loving Cerridwen.
O thou Mighty Cernunnos,
we gather (I stand) before you to ...." *(state intent)*
The Circle is now perfect.

Closing the Circle

When the Circle's work is done, R goes to the East, athame in hand, salutes, and draws a banishing Earth pentagram, saying:
R:
Ye Lords of the Watchtowers of the East, ye Lords of Air, we thank you for attending our rites; and ere ye depart to your beauteous realms, we bid thee Hail and Farewell...

All:
Hail and Farewell! *(R extinguishes Quarter Candle)*

Repeat for the remaining Quarters, addressing each with the titles by which it was invoked.

R thanks and says goodbye to the God and Goddess. (Words To Be Decided.) and extinguishes altar candles.
R then thanks and dismisses any spirits who have gathered.
R:
The Circle is open but unbroken. Merry meet, merry part and merry meet again.

R extinguishes the Presence Lamp, saying:

R:
This rite is ended!
All:
So mote it be!

Consecrating a Sword or Athame

Lay sword (or athame) on pentacle, preferably by, and touching, another, consecrated, weapon. The man asperges them with consecrated salt and water, whereupon the woman picks up the weapon to be consecrated and passes it through the imcense smoke and replaces it on the pentacle. Both lay their right hands upon the weapon and press down, saying:

Both:
I conjure thee, O Sword (Athame), by these Names, Abrahach, Abrach, Abracadabra, that thou servest me for a strength and defence in all magical operations against all mine enemies, visible and invisible. I conjure thee anew by the Holy Name Aradia and by the Holy Name Cernunnos; I conjure thee, O Sword (Athame), that thou servest me for a protection in all adversities; so aid me now!

Again the man asperges, and the woman censes, and the weapon is returned to the pentacle, saying:

Both:
"I conjure thee, O Sword (Athame) of Steel, by the Great Gods and Gentle Goddesses, by the virtue of the heavens, of the stars and of the spirits who preside over them, that thou mayest receive such virtue that I may obtain the end I desire in all things wherein I shall use thee, by the power of Aradia and Cernunnos.

The Partner gives the Fivefold kiss unto the owner of the weapon. If the owner is not present, or if the weapon is jointly owned by them both, the man will give the Fivefold kiss to the woman. For the final kiss upon the mouth, the weapon is suspended between their breasts, held there by the pressure of their embrace. As they seperate, the owner of the weapon immediately uses it to recast the Circle, but without words.

Notes: If possible, lay sword with an already consecrated sword or athame. It should, if possible, be consecrated by both a man and a woman, both of whom are initiated, and both naked as drawn swords. During consecration, press down on sword hard with consecrated sword or athame. If possible partake of Cakes and Wine first, then Magus should sprinkle with water, Witch should cense in First Conjuration, then sprinkle and cense and conjure again with Second Conjuration. If true sword and athame are available, a sword and athame can be consecrated at the same time in which case Magus should press with sword on sword, and Witch with athame on athame, and new sword and athame should touch. In any case, when finished the weapon should be handed to new owner with Fivefold Salute, and should be pressed against the body for a time to get the aura; and it should be in as close connection as possible to the naked body for at least a month, i.e. kept under pillow, etc. Do not allow anyone to touch or handle any of your tools until thoroughly impregnated with your aura; say six months or as near as possible. But a pair working together may own the same tools, which will be impregnated with the aura of both.

Consecrating Other Working Tools
(except a sword or athame)

Place tool on pentacle, and lay right hand(s) on it, saying:
Aradia and Cernunnos, deign to bless and to consecrate this White-Hilted knife (or whatever) that it may obtain the necessary virtue through you for all acts of love and beauty.

Magus sprinkles, Witch censes. Then say:
Aradia and Cernunnos, bless this instrument prepared in your

honour.(if Scourge or Cords, add **... that it may serve for a good cause and end and for your glory.**)

Again Magus sprinkles and Witch censes. (Hand tool to new owner as you would a sword or athame, with a Fivefold Salute.)

All these weapons should be presented to the new owner with Salute. If a Witch Queen, the downward pointing triangle as in the first Degree Initiation. (I rephrased the previous sentence, as the Farrar's version is untypeable. —Sekhet)|End ceremony with Fivefold Salute. The new owner should immediately use the new instruments, i.e. form Circle with Sword, then Athame, incise something with White-Handled knife, exhibit Pentacle to Four Quarters, cense to Four Quarters, use Cords and Scourge; and should continue to use all of them in a Circle as often as possible, for some time.

To mark out a new Circle, stick sword or athame in ground, make a loop in cord, and slip over; then, using cord, mark out a circle, and later mark it with point of sword or athame. Always renew the Circle with sword or athame when about to use, but have it marked so that you always retrace it in same place. Remember the Circle is a protection, a guard against evil influences, and to prevent power created from dispersing; but the Witch, not being evil, may enter and leave freely. But in Art Magic, it is a barrier against forces raised, and when once in the Magus may not leave without great danger. If any great danger is manifested it would be advisable to take refuge in the Circle; but ordinarily sword or athame in hand is perfect protection against anything. Those who make these tools must be purified, clean and properly prepared. When not in use, all tools and weapons should be put away in a secret place; and it is good that this should be near your sleeping place, and that you handle them each night before retiring.

The Charge to New Initiates

O Thou who hast declared intent to become one of us, hear then that which thou must know to do: Single is the race, single of men and of

Gods, from a single source we both draw breath, but a difference of power in everything keeps us apart, for we are as nothing but the Gods stay forever. Yet we can, in greatness of minds, be like the Gods. Though we know not to what goal by day or in the night, Fate has written that we shall run beyond all seas, and earth's last boundaries. Beyond the Spring of night and the Heaven's vast expanse there lies a majesty which is the domain of the Gods. Those who would pass through the Gates of Night and Day to that sweet place, which is between the world of men and the domains of the Lords of the Outer Spaces, know that unless there is truth in thy heart, thy every effort is doomed to failure. **HEAR THEN THE LAW:** That thou lovest all things in nature. That thou walkest humbly in the ways of men and the ways of the Gods. Also it is the law that contentment thou shalt learn, through suffering, and from long years, and from nobility of mind and of purpose. **FOR THE WISE NEVER GROW OLD**. Their minds are nourished by living in the daylight of the Gods and if among the vulgar some discoveries should arise concerning some maxims of thy belief in the Gods so do thou, for the most part, keep silent. For there is a great risk of those who straightaway vomit up that which they hast not digested. And when someone shall say to thee, thou knowest naught and it bites thee naught, then knowest thou that thou hast begun the work. And as sheep do not bring their food to the shepherd to show how much they have eaten but digesting inwardly their provender do bear outwardly wool and milk, even so, do not display the maxims to the vulgar, but rather the works that flow when they are digested.

First Degree Initiation

People:

*   Hierophant (H) (Initiator)
*   Candidiate (C)
*   Hierophant's Working Partner (P)
*   Summoner (S) (Hierophant does his part if S unavailable)
*   High Priestess (HPS) (actually, H or P, depending on gender)

Needs:

* blindfold
* nine foot red cord
* short white cord
* oil
* scourge
* all ordinary esbat requirements

Preparation:

Candidate stands outside Circle to NE, blindfolded and bound by members of the opposite gender. Wrists are bound together in back by middle of a 9 foot red cord, knotted in front at throat with ends hanging down front as cable-tow. A short white cord is fastened to the right ankle with ends tucked in so as not to trip **C** up, saying:

Feet neither bound nor free

HPS casts Circle. Opening ritual is followed to the end of the Drawing Down of the Moon, but the Charge is not yet declaimed.

Summoner fetches Sword (or athame) from the altar, and opens a gate in NE. **S, H,** and **P** face **C** and **S** issues the Challenge:

S:
O thou who standest on the threshold between the pleasant world of men and the dread domains of the Lords of the Outer Spaces, hast thou the courage to make the assay?

Placing point of blade against **C**'s heart, **S** continues:

S:
For I say verily, it were better to rush on my blade and perish, than make the attempt with fear in thy heart.

C:
I have two passwords. Perfect love and perfect trust.

S:
All who have such are doubly welcome.

H:
I give thee a third to pass thee through this dread door.

H grasps C above waist with H's left arm, kisses C on the lips, and swings C into the Circle with H's body, from behind.
S (or P if no S) closes the gate.

H leads C to each Quarter in turn, saying:
H:
Take heed, ye lords of the East (South/West/North) that N... is properly prepared to be initiated a priest[ess] and witch.

H leads C back to centre of Circle (via East) while coven dances around, singing:

Eko, eko Azrak, (etc.)....

... over and over, meanwhile pushing C back and forth among them, until H calls a halt.

Partner then rings bell three times as H turns C to stand before the altar, with C's back to the altar (i.e. facing South if altar is in North). H stands in centre of Circle, facing C (and altar). H says:

H:
In other religions, the postulant kneels, while the priest towers above. But in the Art Magical we are taught to be humble, and we kneel to welcome her [/him] and we say: [kneels]**Blessed be thy feet, which have brought thee in these ways;**[kiss r. foot, then l. foot]
Blessed be thy knees, that shall kneel at the sacred altar;[kiss r. knee, then l. knee]
Blessed be thy womb[/phallus], without which we would not

be;[kiss above pubes]
**Blessed be thy breasts [/breast], erected in beauty [/formed in
strength];**[kiss r. breast, then l. breast]
Blessed be thy lips, that shall utter the sacred names.[kiss on lips]
[rises]

H:
Now we are going to take your measure.
H, aided by another witch of the same gender, stretches a button
thread from the ground by C's foot to crown of C's head and cuts it
there with athame or bolline.
Measure C once about the forehead with the cut thread and knot at
the point of overlap, again about the heart starting from the same end
[knot], and lastly about the hips across the genitals [knot]. The measure is wound and placed upon the altar. H asks:

H:
**Before thou art sworn, art thou ready to pass the ordeal and be
purified?**

C:
I am.

H, aided by another witch of the same gender, helps C to kneel, head
and shoulders bowed forward. The loose ends of the short cord are
unwound and C's ankles bound securely. The cable tow is fastened
to the altar. H fetches scourge from altar as Partner rings bell three
times, saying:

P:
Three.,
H scourges C firmly, but tenderly, thrice.
P says (but doesn't ring bell):
P:
Seven ... Nine ... Twenty-one.,
And each time H scourges C with the number of strokes P has named,
and all should be light, yet firm, save only the very last which may

sting somewhat as a reminder that **H**. has been deliberately restrained. Hierophant then says:

H:
Bravely thou hast passed the test. Art thou ready to swear that thou wilt always be true to the Art?,
C:
I am,
H:
Art thou ever ready to help, protect and defend thy brothers and sisters of the Art, even though it should cost thee thy life.?,
C:
I am,
H:
Then say after me: I, N..., in the presence of the Mighty Ones, do of my own free will and accord, most solemnly swear, without any reservation in me whatever, that I will ever keep secret, and never reveal, the secrets of the Art, except it be to a proper person, properly prepared within a Circle such as I am now in. This I swear by my hopes of a future life, mindful that my measure has been taken; and may my weapons turn against me if I break this my solemn oath,

H and other witch of the same gender help C to feet. P fetches anointing oil and chalice of wine. H moistens fingertip with oil saying:
H:
I hereby sign thee with the Triple Sign. I consecrate thee with oil ...,

H touches moistened finger to just above pubes, right breast, left breast, and above pubes again. H moistens fingertip with wine and anoints the same three places, saying:
H:
I consecrate thee with wine ...,
H:
I consecrate thee with my lips ... [kiss as above] Priest[ess] and witch.,

C is now unbound and the blindfold removed by H and assistant of same gender. New Initiate is welcomed by coven, then presented with the Working Tools. As each tool is named, H takes it from the altar and passes it to the Initiate with a kiss. As each tool is finished with, the assistant takes it from the Initiate [kiss] and replaces it upon the altar. **H** says:

H:
Now I present to thee the Working Tools.,

First, the Magic Sword.,

With this, as with the athame, thou canst form all Magic Circles, dominate, subdue and punish all renellious spirits and daemons, and even pursuade angels and good spirits. With this in thy hand, thou art ruler of the Circle.,

Next I present the Athame. This is the true witch's weapon and has all the powers of the Magic Sword.,

Next I present the White-hilted knife. Its use is to form all instruments used in the Art. It can only be used in a Magic Circle.,

Next I present the Wand. Its use is to call up and control certain angels and genii to whom it would not be meet to use the Magic Sword.,

Next I present the Cup. This is the vessel of the Goddess, the Cauldron of Cerridwen, the Holy Grail of Immortality. From this we drink in comradeship, and in honour of the Goddess,

Next I present the Pantacle. This is for the purpose of calling up appropriate spirits.,

Next I present the Scourge. This is the sign of power and domination. It is also used to cause purification and enlightenment. For it is written: 'To learn you must suffer and be purified.' Art thou willing to suffer to learn?,

C:
I am,

H:
Next and lastly I present the Cords. They are of use to bind the sigils of the Art; also the material basis; also they are necessary in the Oath,

I now salute thee in the name of Aradia, newly made priest[ess] and witch [kiss],

H and P now face the new Initiate and deliver the Charge.
The Initiate may consecrate his athame here; he must consecrate it before using it.
Cakes and Wine
The Initiate is now presented to each Quarter in turn by the Hierophant, saying:
H:
Hear ye Mighty Ones of the East [S./W./N.]; N... has been consecrated priest[ess], witch and hidden child of the Goddess.
to north declaim:
Hear ye Mighty Ones of the North; Boreas, thou guardian of the Northern portals; thou powerful God, thou gentle Goddess; N... .... (etc.)

Close Circle.

A **graduation** party should follow.

Initiation of the Second Degree

HPS casts Circle as usual. Esbat rite is followed to end of Invocation of the Horned God.
Candidate, properly prepared (in centre of Circle), is bound and blindfolded as in the First Degree, but with the addition of a blue cord bound about the knees. Hierophant leads Candidate to each Quarter in turn, proclaiming:

H:

Hear ye O Mighty Ones of the East [S, W, N], N...., a duly consecrated Priest(ess) and Witch is now properly prepared to be made a High Priest and Magus (High Priestess and Witch Queen).
Candidate is returned to center, facing altar. Coven links hands and thrice circle C.
Candidate is now assisted to kneel and rebound securely, facing altar. Hierophant says:

H:

To attain to this sublime degree, it is necessary to suffer and be purified. Art thou willing to suffer to learn?

C:

I am

H:

I purify thee to take this great Oath rightly.
The bell is rung thrice and purification follows: 3, 7, 9, 21 (=40) strokes. Scourge and bell are returned to the altar as Hierophant says:

H:

I now give thee a new name, N.... What is thy name?(giving light smack or push)

C:

My name is N.... (giving light smack or push)
Each member of the Coven in turn gives Candidate a light swat or push, asking:

Each Covener:

What is thy name?(giving light smack or push)
Candidate responds to each with his (her) new name. When all have put the question, all return to their places and **H.** administers the Oath saying:

H:

**Repeat thy new name after me: I, N...., swear upon my mother's
womb, and by mine honour among men and my Brothers and
Sisters of the Art, that I will never reveal, to any at all, any of the
secrets of the Art, except it be to a worthy person, properly prepared, in the center of a Magic Circle such as I am now in; and
that I will never deny the secrets to such a person, if he or she has
been properly vouched for by a Brother or Sister of the Art. All
this I swear by my hopes of salvation, my past lives and my hopes
of future ones to come; and I devote myself and my measure to
utter destruction if I break this my solemn oath.**

Kneeling, H. places left hand under Candidate's knee and right hand
upon his (her) head to form the Magical Link and concentrates long
enough to fully charge **C**, saying:

H:
I will all my power into thee.

Candidate's knees and ankles are now unbound, and he/she is assisted to rise. Hierophant takes up oil and anoints **C**. at pubes, right
breast, left hip, right hip, left breast, and above pubic hair again,
saying:

H:
I consecrate thee with oil.

And again with wine, saying:

H:
I consecrate thee with wine.,?TD>
And lastly kisses Candidate in the same pattern:

H:
**I consecrate thee with my lips, High Priest(ess) and Magus (Witch
Queen).**

The blindfold and cable-tow are now removed and the Initiate is congratulated by coveners.

H. takes up Magic Sword from altar, saying:

H:
You will now show the use of each of the Working Tools in turn.
First the Magic Sword. (S)
(Initiate silently redraws Circle and returns Sword with a S.)

H:
Second the Athame. (S)

(Initiate silently redraws Circle and returns Sword with a S.)

(Initiate again recasts Circle in silence. (S)
&nbps
H:
Third, the White-Hilted Knife. (S)

(Initiate inscribes pentagram in new white candle. S)

H:
Fourth, the Wand. (S)

(Initiate circumambulates presenting Wand to each Quarter. S)

H:
Fifth, the Cup. (S)

(Initiate consecrates wine; may be assisted by H. S)

H:
Sixth, the Pentacle. (S)

(Initiate consecrates cakes; may be assisted by H. S)

H:

Seventh, the Cords. (S)

(Initiate, with help from Partner, binds **H.** as s/he was bound to take this degree. S)

H:
Eighth, the Scourge. For learn, in Witchcraft you must ever give as you receive, but ever triple. So where I gave thee three, return nine; where I gave thee seven, return twenty-one; where I gave thee nine, return twenty-seven; where I gave thee twenty-one, return sixty-three.

(Initiate gives 9, 21, 27, 63 = 120 strokes with Scourge.)

H:
Though hast obeyed the Law. But mark well, when thou receivest good, so equally art thou bound to return good threefold.

H. is unbound and assisted to rise, then leads Initiate to wach Quarter in turn, saying:

H:
Hear ye, Mighty Ones of the East [S. W. N.]: N.... has been duly consecrated High Priest(ess) and Magus (Witch Queen).,**H.** leads Initiate back to center of Circle, saying:

H:
Having learned this far, you must know why the Wicca are called the Hidden Children of the Goddess.
Proceed with the Legend of the Descent of the Goddess. Generally Initiate and Hierophant act the appropriate parts. **H.** appoints Narrator and Guardian.

The Legend of the Descent of the Goddess

roles:

*   Narrator (N)
*   Goddess
*   Lord of Death (D)
*   Guardian(s)

needs:

*   veils, jewellery
*   Horned Crown
*   Sword
*   Scourge

She who will portray the Goddess removes her necklace and places it upon the altar, donning veils and jewellery in its stead.

He who will portray the God dons the Horned Crown and stands before the altar with scourge and blade in the God position.

(S)he who portrays the Guardians bears the Sword.

Each will act out their parts as the Narrator reads:

N:

In Ancient time, out Lord, the Horned One, was as he still is, the Consoler, the Comforter, but men knew him as the dread Lord of Shadows - lonely, stern and just.

Now our Lady the Goddess had never loved, but she would solve all the Mysteries, even the mystery of Death; and so she journeyed to the Underworld.

The Guardians of the Portal challenged her:

Strip off thy garments, lay aside thy jewels; for naught mayest thou bring with thee into this our land.

So she laid down her garments and her jewels, and was bound, as are all who enter the Realms of death, the Mighty One.

Such was her beauty, that Death himself knelt and kissed her feet, saying:

Blessed be thy feet, that have brought thee in these ways. Abide with me; but let me place my cold hand on thy heart.

She replied:

I love thee not. Why dost thou cause all things that I love and take delight in to fade and die?

Death replied:

'Lady 'tis age and fate, against which I am helpless. Age causes all things to wither; but when men die at the end of time, I give them rest and peace, and strength so that they may return. But thou ! Thou art lovely. Return not; abide with me!

But she answered:

I love thee not!

Then said Death:

An thou receivest not my hand upon thy heart, thou must kneel to Death's scourge.

It is fate - better so,

She said. And she knelt, and Death scourged her tenderly.

And she cried:

I feel the pangs of love.

And Death raised her, and said:

Blessed be!

And he gave her the Fivefold kiss, saying:

Thus only mayest thou attain to joy and knowledge.

And he taught her all his Mysteries, and they loved and were one. And she taught him her mystery of the sacred cup which is the cauldron of rebirth. And he gave her the necklace which is the circle of rebirth, and taught her all the magics.

For there are three great events in the life of man: Love, Death and Resurrection in the new body; and Magic controls them all. For to fulfill love you must return again at the same time and place as the loved one, and you must meet, and know, and remember, and love them again. But to be reborn, you must die and be made ready for a new body; and to die, you must be born; and without love, you may not be born; and this is all the Magics.

Initiation of the Third Degree

HPS sits upon the altar, facing South, in the Osiris position. **HP** kneels before her, kisses both knees, extends arms along thighs, and adores. **HP** then fetches filled chalice and celebrates Wine and Cakes. **HP** again kneels before **HPS**, kisses knees and extends arms in adoration as before. Both rise.

HP says:

HP:
Ere I proceed with this sublime rite, I must beg purification at thy hands.

HPS takes up a red cord and binds his arms, then taking up the cable-tow, leads him once about the Circle.

HP kneels facing altar.

Scourge.

HP rises and is unbound whereupon he binds **HPS** as she bound him, leads her about the Circle and scourges her as she kneels before the altar. **HPS** rises and **HP** takes her by the cable-tow to each Quarter in turn, saying:

HP:

Hear ye, Mighty Ones of the East [S, W, N]: the twice consecrated and holy N...., High Priestess and Witch Queen [High Priest and Magus], is properly prepared, and will now proceed to erect the Sacred Altar./FONT>

HP unties **HPS** and says:

HP:

Now again I must beg purification.

HPS binds him, leads him about the Circle and Scourges him kneeling before the altar, as before. He stands and is unbound and says:

HP:

Now I must reveal a great mystery.,

HPS stands vefore altar in God Position.

HP gives her Fivefold Salute. [After he kisses feet, **HPS** opens into Goddess position, still holding scourge and athame].

HPS then sets scourge and athame aside and lies in the middle of the Circle with her head to the East and her womb in the shekinah point. **HP** kneels beside her facing North. [At each point marked (S) below he kisses her womb unless instructed otherwise.] **HP** says:

HP:

Assist me to erect the ancient altar,

At which in days past all worshipped,

The Great Altar of all things;

For in old times, Woman was the altar.
Thus was the altar made and placed;
And the sacred point was the point within the centre of the Circle.
As we have of old been taught that the point within the centre
is the origin of all things,
Therefore should we adore it.   [kiss]
Therefore whom we adore we also invoke,
by the power of the Lifted Lance.[touch phallus]
O Circle of Stars   [kiss]
Whereof our father is but the younger brother   [kiss]
Marvel beyond imagination, soul of infinite space,
Before whom time is bewildered and understanding dark,
Not unto thee may we attain unless thine image be love.   [kiss]
Therefore by seed and root, by stem and bud,
by leaf and flower and fruit, Do we invoke thee,
O Queen of Space, O dew of light,
Continuous one of the heavens   [kiss]
Let it be ever thus, that men speak not of thee as one, but as none;
And let them not speak of thee at all, since thou art continuous.
For thou art the point within the circle   [kiss]
which we adore,   [kiss]
The fount of life without which we would not be,   [kiss]
And in this way are erected the Holy Twin Pillars.
[kiss breasts, left then right]
In beauty and in strength were they erected,
To the wonder and glory of all men.
[If the Great Rite is to be actual, non-participants leave, sealing gate behind.]

HP:
O Secret of Secrets,
That art hidden in the being of all lives,
Not thee do we adore,
For that which adoreth is also thou.
Thou art That, and That am I.   [kiss]
I am the flame that burns in the heart of every man,

And in the core of every star.
I am life, and the giver of life.
Yet therefore is the knowledge of me the knowledge of death.
I am alone, the Lord within ourselves,
Whose name is Mystery of Mysteries.

HP now kisses **HPS** in the Sigil of the Third Degree as follows:

[There's a diagram in the non-computer version which I can't reproduce. It shows the Priestess with the points of the Third Degree Sigil marked on her body. The points are: 1. genitals/womb; 2. right foot; 3. left knee; 4. right knee; 5.left foot; 6. genitals/womb; 7. lips; 8. left breast; 9. right breast; 10. lips.]

and then lays his body gently over hers, saying:

HP:
Make open the path of intelligence between us;
For these truly are the Five Points of Fellowship -
Foot to foot,
knee to knee,
Lance to Grail,
Breast to breast,
Lips to lips.
By the great and holy name Cernunnos;
In the name of Aradia;
Encorage our hearts,
Let the light crystalize itself in our blood,
Fulfilling of us resurrection.
For there is no part of us that is not of the Gods."

.....
HP rises and goes to each Quarter in turn saying:

HP:
Ye Lords of the Watchtowers of the East [S, W, N]; the thrice consecrated High Priestess greets you and thanks you.

The Great Rite

(Alternative Verse Version of Priest's Declamation)

Assist me to build
As the Mighty Ones willed
An altar of praise
From beginning of days.
Thus doth it lie
'Twixt the points of the sky
For thus was it placed
When the Goddess embraced
The Horn'd One, her Lord,
Who taught her the Word
That quickened the womb
And conquered the tomb.
Be thus as of yore,
The shrine we adore, [kiss]
The feast without fail,
The life-giving Grail. [kiss]
Before it uprear
The Miraculous Spear [touches own phallus]
And invoke in this sign
The Goddess divine! [kiss]
Thou who at noon of night doth reign
Queen of the starry realms above,
Not unto thee may we attain
Unless thine image be of love. [kiss]
By moon-ray's silver shaft of power,
By green leaf breaking from the bud,
By seed that springeth into flower,
By life that courseth in the blood, [kiss]
By rushing wind and leaping fire,
By flowing water and green earth,
Pour us the wine of our desire
From out thy Cauldron of Rebirth. [kiss]

Here may we see in vision clear
Thy secret strange unveiled at length,
Thy wondrous Twin Pillars rear
Erect in beauty and in strength. [kisses on the breasts]
Altar of mysteries manifold,
The Sacred Circle's central point
Thus do I sign thee as of old;
With kisses of my lips anoint. [kisses of the Third Degree Sigil]
Open for me the secret way,
The pathway of intelligence
beyond the gates of night and day,
Beyond the bounds of time and sense.
Behold the Mystery aright;
The five true points of fellowship,
Here where the Lance and Grail unite,
And feet and knees and breast and lip.

Esbat Ritual

Needs:

* Everything needed to cast a Circle,
* Wand, Scourge, Priestess' Athame
* Priest, Priestess

Here is the sequence of modules in a standard Esbat ritual.

* Cast Circle
* *(Optional: rare)* Declaim Ancient Call
* Drawing Down the Moon
* Charge
* *(Optional: rare)* HP declaims Ancient Call
* Great God Cernunnos Invocation (generally omitted if Drawing Down the Sun)
* Witches' Rune (or other circle chant, eg. Ancient Call)
* Cone of Power

*   *Insert optional Circle work here (eg. Sabbat ritual)*
*   Wine Blessing
*   Cake Blessing
*   *Relax and chat; Coven business discussion, teaching, etc.*
*   Close Circle

The Witches' Rune

Darksome night and shining moon,
Hearken to the witches' rune.
East, then south, west then north,
Here come I to call the forth.

Earth and water, air and fire,
Work ye unto my desire.
Wand and Pentacle and Sword
Hearken ye unto my word.

Cords and Censer, Scourge and Knife,
Waken all ye into life.
Powers of the Witches Blade,
Come ye as the charm is made.

Queen of Heaven, Queen of Hell,
Lend your aid unto the spell.
Horned Hunter of the Night,
Work my will by magic rite.

By all the power of land and sea,
As I do will, so mote it be.
By all the might of moon and sun,
Chant the spell and be it done.

Darksome night and shining moon,
East, then south, west then north,
Hearken to the witches' rune.

Here come I to call the forth.

instead of in couplets); this is unlikely be found in its original form in a "standard" North American Gardnerian or Alexandrian BOS. (It seems to have been changed fairly early in its history.)

* **See Janet and Stewart Farrar's** *The Witches' Way* **(as usual) for historical details.**
* **See the following (and many more) for published versions:**
* **Janet and Stewart Farrar** *The Witches' Way*
* **Janet and Stewart Farrar** *Eight Sabbats For Witches*
* **Stewart Farrar** *What Witches Do*
* *The Grimoire of Lady Sheba*

The Charge

(prose version)

HP stands to HPS's left; both face Coven.

HP:
Listen to the words of the Great Mother; she who of old was also called among men Artemis, Astarte, Athene, Dione, Melusine, Aphrodite, Cerridwen, Cybele, Arianrhod, Isis, Dana, Bride and by many other names. At her altars the youth of Lacedaemon in Sparta made due sacrifice.

HPS:
Whenever ye have need of anything, once in the month, and better it be when the moon is full, then shall ye assemble in some secret place and adore the spirit of me, who am Queen of all the witcheries. There shall ye assemble, ye who are fain to learn all sorcery, yet have not won its deepest secrets; to these will I teach things that are yet unknown. And ye shall be free from slavery; and as a sign that ye be really free, ye shall be naked in your rites; and ye shall dance, sing, feast, make music and love, all in my praise. For mine is the ecstasy of the spirit, and mine also is joy on earth; for my law is love unto all beings. Keep pure your

highest ideal; strive ever towards it; let naught stop you or turn you aside. For mine is the secret door which opens upon the Land of Youth, and mine is the cup of the wine of life, and the Cauldron of Cerridwen, which is the Holy Grail of immortality. I am the Gracious Goddess, who gives the gift of joy unto the heart of man. Upon earth, I give the knowledge of the spirit eternal; and beyond death, I give peace and freedom and reunion with those who have gone before. Nor do I demand aught in sacrifice; for behold, I am the Mother of all living, and my love is poured out upon the earth.

HP:

Hear ye the words of the Star Goddess; she in the dust of whose feet are the hosts of heaven, and whose body encircles the Universe.

HPS:

I who am the beauty of the green earth, and the white Moon among the stars, and the mystery of the waters, and the desire of the heart of man, call unto thy soul. Arise, and come unto me. For I am the soul of nature, who gives life to the universe. From me all things proceed, and unto me all things must return; and before my face, beloved of Gods and of men, let thine innermost divine self be enfolded in the rapture of the infinite. Let my worship be within the heart that rejoiceth; for behold, all acts of love and pleasure are my rituals. And therefore let there be beauty and strength, power and compassion, honour and humility, mirth and reverence within you. And thou who thinkest to seek for me, know thy seeking and yearning shall avail thee not unless thou knowest the mystery; that if that which thou seekest thee findest not within thee, thou wilt never find it without thee. For behold, I have been with thee from the beginning; and I am that which is attained at the end of desire.

Athena Gardner

The Charge

(verse version)

HPS:
All ye assembled in my sight,
Bow before my spirit bright.
Aphrodite, Arionrhod,
Lover of the Horned God,
Mighty Queen of Witchery and night.
Morgan, Etoine, Nisene,
Diana, Bridgid, Melusine,
Am I named of old by men.
Artemis and Cerridwen,
Hell's dark mistress, Heaven's Queen.
Ye who would ask of me a rune,
Or who would ask of me a boon,
Meet me in some secret glade,
Dance my round in greenwood shade,
By the light of the full moon.
In a place wild and lone,
Dance about mine altar stone;
Work my holy mystery.
Ye who are feign to sorcery,
I bring ye secrets yet unknown.
No more shall ye know slavery,
Who give true worship unto me.
Ye who tread my round on Sabbat night,
Come ye all naked to the rite,
In token that ye be really free.
I teach ye the mystery of rebirth,
Work ye my mysteries in mirth.
Heart joined to heart and lip to lip,
Five are the points of fellowship,
That bring ye ecstasy on earth,
For I am the circle of rebirth.
I ask no sacrifice, but do bow,

No other Law but love I know,
By naught but love may I be known.
All things living are mine own,
From me they come, to me they go.

Drawing Down the Moon

Needs:

*   Wand, Scourge, Priestess' Athame
*   Priest, Priestess

Follows: Casting Circle, Witches' Rune
Next: The Charge

HPS stands in God position in N. before altar, holding scourge and athame.
Coveners are in S. facing altar.
HP kneels before **HPS** and salutes her with the Fivefold kiss (as he kisses her womb, she opens into blessing position).

HP again kneels before **HPS** who stands in Goddess positon (right foot slightly forward). **HP** invokes the Goddess, saying:

HP:
I invoke thee and call upon thee,
Mighty Mother of us all,   (touch right breast)
bringer of all fruitfulness;   (touch left breast)
by seed and root,   (touch womb)
by stem and bud,   (touch right breast)
by leaf and flower and fruit,
by life and love   (touch womb)
do I invoke   (raising wand)
thee to descend upon the body
of this thy servant and priestess.

Here, speak with her tongue,
touch with her hands,
kiss with her lips,
that thy servants may be fulfilled.
As he invokes, **HP** touches **HPS** gently with wand upon r. breast, l. breast, womb and upon the same three places again.

As he finishes the invocation, he spreads his arms in adoration (still kneeling) and says:

HP:
Hail, Aradia ! From the Amalthean Horn
Pour forth thy store of love; I lowly bend
Before thee, I adore thee to the end,
With loving sacrifice thy shrine adorn.
Thy foot is to my lip [kiss], my prayers upborne
Upon the rising incense smoke; then spend
Thine ancient love, O Mighty One, descend
To aid me, who without thee am forlorn.

HP stands and takes a step back. All adore in silence as **HPS** traces invoking Earth pentagram in air before them with athame, saying:

HPS:
Of the Mother, darksome and divine,
Mine the scourge, and mine the kiss,
The five-point star of love and bliss -
Here I charge you, in this sign.

This completes Drawing Down the Moon. **HPS** and **HP** now face the Coven and deliver the Charge.

The Ancient Call

May be used as a circle chant, or declaimed (generally by **HP**) generally either before the Great God Cernunnos Invocation, or before the Witches' Rune.

HP raises his arms wide and says:

HP: (First three verses are sometimes dropped)
Eko, Eko, Azarak
Eko, Eko, Zamilak
Eko, Eko, Cernunnos,
Eko, Eko, Aradia

Eko, Eko, Azarak
Eko, Eko, Zamilak
Eko, Eko, Cernunnos,
Eko, Eko, Aradia

Eko, Eko, Azarak
Eko, Eko, Zamilak
Eko, Eko, Cernunnos,
Eko, Eko, Aradia

Bagabi laca bachabe
Lamac cahi achababe
Karelyos!
Lmaca lamac bachalyos
Cabahagi sabalyos
Baryolas!
Lagoz atha cabyolas
Samahac atha famyolas
Hurrahya!

HPS and coven repeat:
Hurrahya!

Great God Cernunnos Invocation

HPS and **HP** turn to salute altar with the Horned God's salute as **HP** says:

HP:
Great God Cernunnos, return to earth again!
Come at my call and show thyself to men.
Shepherd of Goats, upon the wild hill's way,
Lead thy lost flock from darkness into day.
Forgotten are the ways of sleep and night -
Men seek for them whose eyes have lost the light.
Open the door, the door which hath no key,
The door of dreams, whereby men come to thee.
O Mighty Stag, O answer to me!

HPS & HP say:

Both:
Akhera goiti
- akhera beiti! (lowering their hands)

Cone of Power

HP leads a ring dance deosil about **HPS** who stands in the center. Coveners are arranged man and woman alternately, facing inwards and holding hands (left plams up, right palms down). All dance and chant either the Witches' Rune or the call of the ancient Mysteries:

All:
Eo, Evohe!

Dance and chant faster and faster until **HPS** senses that the time is right, whereupon she calls:

HPS:

Down!

All shall drop to the ground in a circle facing the **HPS**. If there is coven work to be done, now is the appropriate time to do it. Or a meditation upon the Moon's season, or such other matter as may be fitting or needful. At an esbat Wine and Cakes will follow, but at a Sabbat the Great Rite comes first.

Wine Blessing

Follows: working part of Esbat Circle (any worship Circle)

HPS stands in God position before altar. **HP** fills a Chalice with red wine and offers it up to her from his knees.

HPS takes Athame between her palms and holds it above the Chalice.

HP:
As the athame is to the male,
HPS:
so the cup is to the female;
Both:
and conjoined they bring blessedness.

Laying athame aside, **HPS** accepts cup of **HP** (kiss), sips and returns it to him (kiss) who also sips and arises to pass it to a woman (kiss) to sip and hence from woman to man (kiss) and man to woman (kiss) about the Circle. If more work is to be done, the cup makes the round but once and is returned to the altar, else it is replaced in the center of the Circle.

Cake Blessing

Follows: Wine Blessing

To consecrate cakes, **HPS** picks up athame again as **HP** kneels before her, holding up the dish of cakes. **HPS** draws invoking pentagram of earth over the cakes saying:

HPS:
O Queen, most secret, bless this food unto our bodies; bestowing health, wealth, strength, joy and peace, and that fulfillment of love which is perfect happiness.

All sit as the cakes are passed around as was the wine.

HP refills cup and offers it to **HPS**, inviting her to join them. When done relaxing and chatting, close the Circle.

Invocation to the Horned God

By the flame that burneth bright,
O Horned One!
We call thy name into the night,
O Ancient One!
Thee we invoke by the Moon-led sea,
By the standing stone and the twisted tree.
Thee we invoke, where gather Thine own.
By the nameless shore, forgotten and lone.
Come where the round of the dance is trod,
Horn and Hoof of the Goat Foot God!
By moonlit meadow, on dusky hill,
Where the haunted wood is hushed and still,
Come to the charm of the chanted prayer,
As the Moon bewitches the midnight air.
Evoke thy powers that potent bide
In shining stream and the secret tide,
In fiery flame by starlight pale,
In shadowy host that rides the gale.
And by the ferndrakes, faerie haunted,
Of forests wild and woods enchanted.
Come, O Come!

To the heartbeat's drum!
Come to us who gather below,
When the broad white Moon is climbing slow.
Through the stars to the heavens' height,
We hear thy hoofs on the wind of night!
As black tree branches shake and sigh,
By joy and terror we know thee nigh.
We speak the spell thy power unlocks,
At Solstice Sabbath and Equinox!"

Besom Chant

Besom, besom long and lithe
Made from ash and willow withe
Tied with thongs of willow bark
In running stream at moonset dark.
With a pentagram indighted
As the ritual fire is lighted;
Sweep ye circle, deosil,
Sweep out evil, sweep out ill,
Make the round of the ground
Where we do the Lady's will.

Besom, besom, Lady's broom
Sweep out darkness, sweep out doom
Rid ye Lady's hallowed ground
Of demons, imps and Hell's red hound;
Then set ye down on Her green earth
By running stream or Mistress' hearth,
'Till called once more on Sabbath night
To cleans once more the dancing site.

Yule

Preparation:
Let all be properly prepared and purified.
In the centre (or just south of centre) of the Circle stands the Cauldron of Cerridwen wreathed about with pine boughs, holly, ivy and mistletoe and therein is laid a balefire of nine woods: rowan, apple, elder, holly, pine, cedar, juniper, poplar and dogwood.
The altar is decorated as is the Cauldron and bears two red candles as well as an unlit red candle or torch for each covener present. There should be no other light except the altar candles and those about the Circle.

HP casts the Circle, calling forth the Ancient Ones to bear witness.

HP draws down the moon upon the **HPS** and then lights the balefire.

HP then moves to the north, before the altar, as the **HPS** stands in the south with the coveners in a circle, alternately man and woman, about the Cauldron between them.

The circle now moves slowly deosil once about the Circle. As each passes the **HPS** they kiss her upon the cheek; as they pass the **HP**, he hands each one a candle which is lit from the balefire.

Coveners dance slowly deosil as the **HP** calls:

HP:
Queen of the Moon, Queen of the Sun,
Queen of the Heavens, Queen of the Stars,
Queen of the Waters, Queen of the Earth,
Bring to us the Child of Promise!
It is the Great Mother who gives birth to Him;
It is the Lord of Life who is born again.
Darkness and tears are set aside when the Sun shall come up early.
Golden Sun of hill and mountain,
Illumine the land, illumine the world,

Illumine the seas, illumine the rivers,
Sorrows be laid, joy to the world!
Blessed be the Great Goddess,
Without beginning, without ending,
Everlasting to eternity.
Io Evoe! Heh! Blessed be!

All raise their tapers high and repeat twice the last line.
HPS joins the dance, leading it with a quieter rhythm.

The burning cauldron is pushed into the centre and the dancers jump over it in man and woman couples. The last couple over the fire should be well purified, three times each, and may pay an amusing forfeit as the **HPS** may ordain.

Cakes and wine follows and, after the Circle has been closed, much merriment, feasting, dancing and games.

Candlemas

The **HPS**, carrying the Wand, leads the coveners with a dance step to the chosen site.
The Volta Dance follows: in other words, lively dancing in couples.
HPS casts the Circle in the usual way.
HP then enters the Circle, with a Sword in his right hand and a Wand in his left. He lays these on the altar.
HP now salutes the HPS with the Fivefold Kiss.
She says Blessed be and gives him the Fivefold Kiss in return.

HP assumes the god position before the altar as the HPS invokes:
HPS:
Dread Lord of Death and Resurrection,
Of Life, and the Giver of Life;
Lord within ourselves, whose name is Mystery of Mysteries;
Encourage our hearts,
Let the Light crystallize itself in our blood,

Fulfilling us of resurrection;
For there is no part of us that is not of the Gods.
Descend, we pray thee, upon thy servant and priest.

Any initiations to be done are done at this point.
The ceremony of Cakes and Wine follows.
The Great Rite is done if at all possible.
Feasting, dancing and games follow the closing of the ritual.

Vernal Equinox (Eostar)

Preparation:
A Symbol of the Wheel is on the altar, flanked with burning candles, or with fire in some form - torches, or small tripods with fire in their cups.
The Symbol of the Wheel may be a plain disc, or an eight spoked wheel, or the pentacle. Alex and Maxine Sanders used a circular mirror with a broad frame, also circular, decorated as a twelve-pointed star.
In the centre of the Circle is either a cauldron full of inflammable material, or (out of doors) a bonfire ready to be lit.

HPS casts the Circle.

HPS then stands in the West, and the **HP** in the East, both with carrying wands.
HPS:
We kindle this fire today
In the presence of the Holy Ones,
Without malice, without jealousy, without envy,
Without fear of aught beneath the Sun
But the High Gods.
Thee we invoke, O Light of Life;
Be thou a bright flame before us,
Be thou a guiding star above us,
Be thou a smooth path beneath us;

Kindle thou within our hearts
A flame of love for our neighbours,
To out foes, to our friends, to our kindred all,
To all men on the broad earth;
O merciful Son of Cerridwen,
From the lowliest thing that liveth,
To the Name which is highest of all.

HPS then draws invoking pentagram before the **HP** and then hands the Wand to him, together with the scourge.

The Maiden strikes a light and hands it to the High Priest, who lights the cauldron or bonfire. He (carrying a wand) and the High Priestess (carrying a sistrum) lead the dance, with the rest following in couples. Each couple must leap over the fire. The last couple over the fire before it goes out must be well purified. The man must then give a fivefold kiss to each of the women, as the woman to the men, or any other penalty the **HPS** shall decide.

Cakes and wine shall follow.

Beltane

Preparation:
Two white candles are on the altar with a wreath of spring flowers. Quarter candles are green.

HPS leads the coven, riding poles if possible, about the Covenstead with a quick, trotting step, singing:

All:
O do not tell the priests of our Art,
For they would call it sin;
But we will be in the woods all night,
A-conjuring summer in.
And we bring you good news by word of mouth,
For woman, cattle and corn,

For the sun is coming up from the south
With oak and ash and thorn.

A ring dance follows after which the High Priestess casts the Circle.
High Priest draws down the Moon upon the High Priestess.
All are purified in sacrifice before Her.
She then purifies the High Priest at her own hands.
All Partake of Cakes and Wine followed by feasting and dancing and
singing and the Great Rite, if at all possible, in token or truly.

Midsummer

The cauldron, filled with water and decorated with flowers, is placed
before the altar. **HPS** casts the Circle and then stands before the Caul-
dron, wand upraised. **HP** stands in North behind the altar; coven is in
a circle, facing inwards, alternately man and woman. **HPS** says:
HPS:
Great One of Heaven, Power of the Sun,
We invoke thee in thy ancient names -
Michael, Balin, Arthur, Lugh, Herne;
Come again as of old into this thy land.
Lift up thy shining spear of light to protect us.
Put to flight the powers of darkness.
Give us fair woodlands and green fields,
Blooming orchards and ripening corn.
Bring us to stand upon thy hill of vision,
And show us the lovely realms of the Gods.

HPS traces an invoking pentagram upon the **HP** with her wand. He
comes desoil about the altar picking up his own wand and the scourge.
He plunges the wand into the cauldron and holds it up, saying:

HP:
The Spear to the Cauldron, the Lance to the Grail, Spirit to Flesh,
Man to Woman, Sun to Earth.

Saluting **HPS** with wand, he joins the Coven in their circle. **HPS** picks up a sprinkler and stands by the cauldron, saying:

HPS:
Dance ye about the Cauldron of Cerridwen, the Goddess, and be ye blessed with the touch of this Ccnsecrated water; even as the Sun, the Lord of Life, ariseth in his strength in the sign of the Waters of Life.

HP leads a slow circle dance deosil about the Cauldron. As each passes, **HPS** sprinkles them with water from it.

Cakes and wine follow and dances, rites and games as the **HPS** shall direct. A balefire may be lit and leaped.

Lammas

Poles should be ridden in a ring dance about the Covenstead. And sing the Ancient Call. The casting of the Circle follows. **HPS** traces the Five Point Star before the Coven saying:

HPS:
O Mighty Mother of us all, Mother of all things living, give us fruit and grain, flocks and herds and children to the tribe, that we may be mighty. By thy Rosey Love, do thou descend upon thy servant and priestess here.
HPS draws down the Moon upon herself and all salute Her.
After a brief silence for contemplation, the Ceremony of Cakes and Wine follows.

Autumnal Equinox

The altar is decorated with the symbols of autumn: pine-cones, oak sprigs, acorns, ears of grain, etc.

After the Circle has been cast, the coven stands in a ring facing in-wards, men and women alternately. The High Priest stands to the west of the altar and the High Priestess to the east, facing each other. The High Priestess recites:

HPS:
Farewell, O Sun, ever-returning Light,
The hidden God, who ever yet remains,
Who now departs into the Land of Youth
Through the Gates of Death
To dwell enthroned, the Judge of Gods and men,
The horned leader of the hosts of air -
Yet even as he stands unseen about the Circle,
So dwelleth he within the secret seed -
The seed of newly-ripened grain, the seed of flesh;
Hidden in earth, the marvellous seed of the stars.
In him is Life, and Life is the Light of man.
That which never was born, and never dies.
Therefore the wise weep not, but rejoice.

HPS hands **HP** the wand, and picks up a sistrum; they lead the dance three times round the altar.

The Candle Game is played, followed by cakes and wine and any other games the High Priestess decides on.

Hallowmas

Preparation:

* Balefire in centre.
* Two black candles upon the altar.
* A red candle in each of the Quarters.
* A wreath of autumn flowers and the crown of the Horned One are upon the altar.

All Coveners are properly prepared, naked and bound.
All are purified by the scourge.

HPS erects the Circle. The **HP** says:

HP:
O Gods, beloved of us all,
bless this our Sabbat that we,
thy humble worshippers,
may meet in love, joy and bliss.
Bless our rites this night
with the presence of our departed kin.

Facing north with arms upraised, coveners hand-linked in a semi-circle behind him, the **HP** invokes the Horned One.

HPS bearing a priapus wand then leads the Coven in a meeting dance, slowly, to the Witches' Rune. **HP** gives each an unlit candle and brings up the rear of the dance. The candles are each lit from the balefire before the outward spiral.

When it is done the HPS assumes the Goddess position saying:

HPS:
Dread Lord of the Shadows, God of Life and Bringer of Death! Yet as the knowledge ofthee is Death, open wide, I pray thee, the gates through which all must pass. Let our dear ones, who have gone before, return this night to make merry with us. And when our time comes, as it must, O thou the Comforter, the Consoler, the Giver of Peace and rest, we will enter thy realms gladly and unafraid; for we know that when rested and refreshed among our dear ones, we will be reborn again by thy grace, and the grace of the Lady Cerridwen. Let it be in the same place and the same time as our beloved ones, and may we meet, and know, and remember, and love them again ! Descend, we pray thee, on thy High Priest and Servant, N....

HPS goes to the **HP** and, with wand, draws the five-point star upon his breast and upon the crown of the Horned God. **HP** kneels and **HPS places the crown upon his head. Fresh incense is cast into the thurible. HPS strikes the bell and HP says:**

HP:
Hear ye my witches,
Welcome to our Great Sabbat.
Welcome we the spirits
Of our departed kin.

HPS strikes bell. Witches walk slowly around the Circle.
HPS fills chalice with wine and hands it to HP who drinks and then says:

HP:
In humility, as the Horned One asks,
I bid my witches drink.

HP takes chalice to first witch, giving it with his right hand whilst taking the taper with his left (kiss), then extinguishing the taper before accepting back the chalice. Repeat with each witch present. HP then says:

HP:
Listen, my witches, to the words of the Horned One, Drink, dance and be merry in the presence of the Old Gods and the spirits of our departed kin.

Coveners partake of cakes and wine.
Dances and games follow closing of Circle.
Great Rite if at all possible by High Priestess and High Priest if no other.
Merry meet, merry part.

Earth

Goddess Aspect: Crone
Astrological Rulers: Venus, Saturn
Keys: Law Principle, Solidity, Auriel ("Lord of Awe")
Rules: Birth & death, body, growth, nature, stones & metals, material things, caves, chasms, silence, graves, fields, Sanguine; Sensation; calm, imperturbable
Virtues: Strength, endurance, commitment, responsibility, thoroughness, practicality, wisdom, patience, sense of timing
Vices: Dullness, lack of conscience, melancholy, boredom, inertia, stagnation, hoarding of resources (including information)
Season: Yule
Time of Day: Midnight
Direction: North
Wind: Boreas
Colour: Green
Symbols: Oak, rock crystal, salt, bull or cow, stag, grains, comfrey, ivy
Tools: Pentacle, altar stone (body of Anima Mundi)
Spirits: Gnomes under Gob (friendly & easy to reach, teach access to own depths & caverns & how to mine & work the vein of gold therein)
Shortage: Spaciness, hyper-activity, instability
Excess: Body heaviness, general lack of energy, inertia, etc.

Water

Goddess Aspect: Mother
Astrological Rulers: Venus, Moon
Keys: Love Principle, Fertility, Gabriel (turns force into form)
Rules: Emotions, love, sorrow, courage, astral planes, clairvoyance, tides, oceans, pools, streams, wells, womb Melancholic; Feeling;

strong, excitatory
Virtues: Compassion, tranquility, tenderness, forgiveness, modesty, fluidity in creativity, receptivity, influence
Vices: Self-indulgence, negligence, cowardice, indifference, instability, moodiness, infatuation, easily put upon, delusions
Season: Autumn
Time of Day: Sunset
Direction: West
Wind: Zephyrus
Colour: Blue
Symbols: Willlow, dolphin, fish, water snakes, sea birds, myrrh, ferns, rushes
Tool: Cup
Spirits: Undines under Neksa (elusive at first, flowing & difficult to understand, watch politely and learn)

Fire

Goddess Aspect: Temptress
Astrological Rulers: Sun, Mars, Jupiter
Keys: Light Principle, Action, Michael (victor over ignorance)
Rules: Force, energy, spirit, heat, mental plane, blood, sap, life, will, surgery, destruction, purification, hearth fires, volcanoes, explosions, Choleric; Intuitive; lively
Virtues: Courageous, self-assertive, chivalrous, enthusiastic, passionate, experienced, virile
Vices: Self-centred, ruthless, fanaticism, vindictiveness, anger, hatred
Season: Midsummer
Time of Day: Noon
Direction: South
Wind: Notus
Colour: Red
Symbols: Fire opal, almond (in flower), garlic, hibiscus, pepper, olibanum

Tools: Scourge, sword, athame
Spirits: Salamanders under Djinn (elusive & hostile, teach power over fire & energy)
Shortage: Body heavy or chilled, thoughts drag-gy, unenthusiastic
Excess: Hot, hyper, flitting thoughts, insomnia, anger, snappishness
NOTES

Air

Goddess Aspect: Maiden
Astrological Rulers: Jupiter, Mercury
Keys: Life Principle, Intellect, Raphael (instructor, traveller, healer)
Rules: Mind, essential qualities, spiritual plane, knowledge, abstract learning, theories, windy or high places, breath, speech, Phlegmatic; Thinking; weak inhibitory
Virtues: Gregarious, diligent, optimistic, dexterity, joie-de-vivre, persuasive, friendly, healthy, knowledgeable
Vices: Frivolity, boasting, absent mindedness, rootless, easily distracted, loquacious, tends to intellectualize emotions (rather than experience them)
Season: Spring
Time of Day: Sunrise
Direction: East
Wind: Eurus
Colour: Yellow
Symbols: Topaz, galbanum, aspen, frankincense, vervain, birds, eagle & hawk
Tools: Wand, censer (arrow stabs air & conveys message Outer to Inner)
Spirits: Sylphs under Paralda (very hard to see & know, teach mind control and how to level out your thinking processes)
Shortage: Mind blank, shortness of breath, non-comprehension of known data
Excess: "Gas bloat", inability to focus attention, "spacey" thoughts
  NOTES

The Witches' Wheel

```
Winter                    Candlemas              Spring
Solstice                    Feb 2                Equinox
Dec 22                                           March 21

    Black              Drugs           Citrine
              Trance     &
                        Wine

    Meditation  Winter  Spring    Dance
Samhain                                          Beltane
Oct 31                                           May 1

              Fall    Summer
    Cords                      Great
                               Rite

                       Spells
              Scourge    &
    Russet             Rites         Olive

Autumn                   Lammas              Summer
Equinox                   Aug 1              Solstice
Sep 21                                       June 22
```

The Eight Paths

The Ways of Making Magic

The [eight pointed asterisk] sign on the Athame is said to represent, among other things, the Eight Paths which all lead to the Center and the Eight Ways of Making magic, and these are:

1.   Meditation or concentration.
2.   Chants, Spells, Invocations. Invoking the Goddess, etc.
3.   Projection of the Astral Body, or Trance.
4.   Incense, Drugs, Wine, etc. Any potion which aids to release the Spirit.

5. Dancing
6. Blood control. Use of the Cords.
7. The Scourge.
8. The Great Rite.

You can combine many of these ways to produce more power.

To practice the Art successfully, you need the following five things:

1. Intention. You must have the absolute will to succeed, the firm belief that you can do so and the determination to win through against all obstacles.
2. Preparation. You must be properly prepared.
3. Invocation. The Mighty Ones must be invoked.
4. Consecration. The Circle must be properly cast and consecrated and you must have properly consecrated tools.
5. Purification. You must be purified.

Hence there are 5 things necessary before you can start, and then 8 Paths or Ways leading to the Centre. For instance, you can combine 4, 5, 6, 7, and 8 together in one rite; or 4, 6 and 7 together with 1 and 2, or with 3 perhaps. The more ways you can combine, the more power you produce.

It is not meet to make offering of less than two score lashes to the Goddess, for here be a mystery. The fortunate numbers be 3, 7, 9 and thrice 7 which be 21. And these numbers total two score, so a less perfect or fortunate number would not be a perfect prayer. Also the Fivefold Salute be 5, yet it be 8 kisses; for there be 2 feet, 2 knees and 2 breasts. And five times 8 be two score. Also there be 8 Working Tools and the Pentacle be 5; and five eights be two score.

(Note: 8 plus 5 equals 13. 8 multipled by 5 equals 40.)

Power

Power is latent in the body and may be drawn out and used in various ways by the skilled. But unless confined in a circle it will be swiftly dissapated. Hence the importance of a poroperly constructed circle. Power seems to exude from the body via the skin and possibly from the orifices of the body; hence you should be properly prepared. The slightest dirt spoils everything, which shows the importance of thorough cleanliness.

The attitude of mind has great effect, so only work with a spirit of reverence. A little wine taken and repeated during the ceremony, if necessary, helps to produce the power. Other strong drinks or drugs may be used, but it is necessary to be very moderate, as if you are confused, even slightly, you cannot control the power you evoke.

The simplest way is by dancing and singing monotonous chants, slowly at first and gradually quickening the tempo until giddiness ensues. Then the calls may be used, or even wild and meaningful shrieking produces power. But this method inflames the mind and renders it difficult to control the power, though control may be gained through practice. The scourge is a far better way, for it stimulates and excites both body and soul, yet one easily retains control. The Great Rite is far the best. It releases enormous power, but the conditions and circumstances make it difficult for the mind to maintain control at first. It is again a matter of practice and the natural strength of the operator's will and in a lesser degree those of his assistants. If, as of old, there were many trained assistants present and all wills properly attuned, wonders occur.

Sorcerors chiefly used the blood sacrifice; and while we hold this to be evil we cannot deny that this method is very efficient. Power flashes forth from newly shed blood, instead of slowly exuding as by our method. The victim's terror and anguish add keenness and quite a small animal can yield enormous power. The great difficulty is in the human mind controlling the power of the lower animal mind. But sorcerors claim they have methods for effecting this and that the difficulty disappears the higher the animal used and when the victim is human disappears entirely. (The practice is an abomination, but it is so.)

Priests know this well; and by their auto-da-fe's, with the victim's pain and terror (the fires acting much the same as circles), obtained enormous power.

Of old the Flagellants certainly evoked power, but through not being confined by a circle most was lost. The amount of power raised was so great and continuous that anyone with knowledge could direct and use it; and it is most probable that the classical and heathen sacrifices were used in the same way. There are whispers that when the human victim was a willing sacrifice, with his mind directed on the Great Work and with highly skilled assistants, wonders ensued - but of this I would not speak.

Properly Prepared

Naked, but sandals (not shoes) may be worn. For initiation, tie hands behind back, pull up to small of back and tie ends in front of throat, leaving a cable-tow to lead by, hanging down in front. (Arms thus form a triangle at back.) When initiate is kneeling at altar, the cable-tow is tied to a ring in the altar. A short cord is tied like a garter round the initiate's left leg above the knee, with ends tucked in. Another is tied round right ankle and ends tucked in so as to be out of the way while moving about. These cords are used to tie feet together while initiate is kneeling at the altar and must be long enough to do this firmly. Knees must also be firmly tied. This must be carefully done. If the aspirant complains of pain the bonds must be loosened slightly; always remember the object being to retard the blood flow enough to induce a trance state. This involves slight discomfort; but great discomfort prevents the trance state, so it is best to spend some little time loosening and tightening the bonds until they are just right. The aspirant alone can tell you when this is so. This, of course, does not apply to the initiation, as then no trance is desired; but for the purpose of ritual it is good that the initiates be bound firmly enough to feel they are absolutely helpless but without discomfort.

The Measure (in the First Degree) is taken thus:

Height, round neck, across the heart and across the genitals. The old custom is, if anyone were guilty of betraying the secrets, their measure was buried at midnight in a boggy place, with curses that "as the measure rots, so they will rot."

The Meeting Dance

The Maiden should lead. A man should place both hands on her waist, standing behind her, and alternate men and women do the same, the Maiden leading and they dance following her. She at last leads them into a right-hand spiral. When the center is reached (and this had better be marked by a stone) she suddenly turns round and dances back, kissing each man as she comes to him. All men and women turn likewise and dance back, men kissing women and women kissing men. All in time to music, it is a merry game, but must be practiced to be done well. Note, the musician should watch the dancers and make the music fast or slow as is best. For the beginners it should be slow, or there will be confusion. It is most excellent to get people to know each other at big gatherings.

Of Calls

Of old there were many chants and songs used, especially in the dances. Many of these have been forgotten by us here; but we know they used cries of IAU, HAU, which seems much like the cry of the ancients: EVO or EAVOE. Much dependeth upon the pronunciation if this be so. In my youth when I heard the cry IAU it seemed to me to be AEIOU, or rather HAAEE IOOUU or AA EE IOOOOUU. This may be but the way to prolong it to make it fit for a call; but it suggests that these may be the initials of an invocation, as AGLA used to be. And of sooth the whole Hebrew Alphabet is said to be such and for this reason is recited as a most powerful charm. At least this is certain, these cries during the dances do have a powerful effect, as I myself have seen.

Other calls are: IEHOUA and EHEIE. Also HO HO HO ISE

81

ISE ISE.

IEO VEO VEO VEO VEOV OROV OV OVOVO may be a spell, but it is more likely to be a call. 'Tis like the EVOE EVOE of the Greeks and the Heave Ho! of sailors. Emen hetan and Ab hur, ab hus seem calls; as Horse and hattock, horse and go! Horse and pellatis, ho, ho, ho!

Thout, tout a tout tout, throughout and about and Rentum tormentum are probably mispronounced attempts at a forgotten formula, though they may have been invented by some unfortunate being tortured, to evade telling the real formula.

NOTES

The Cone of Power

This was the old way. The circle was marked out and people stationed to whip up the dancers. A fire or candle was within it in the direction where the object of the rite was supposed to be. Then all danced round until they felt they had raised enough power. If the rite was to banish they started deosil and finished tuathil, so many rounds of each. Then they formed a line with linked hands and rushed towards the fire shouting the thing they wanted. They kept it up 'til they were exhausted or until someone fell in a faint, when they were said to have taken the spell to its destination.

Of the Ordeal of the Art Magical

Learn of the spirit that goeth with burdens that have not honour, for 'tis the spirit that stoopeth the shoulders and not the weight. Armour is heavy, yet it is a proud burden and a man standeth upright in it. Limiting and constraining any of the senses serves to increase the concentration of another. Shutting the eyes aids the hearing. So the binding of the Initiate's hands increases the mental perception, while the scourge increaseth the inner vision. So the Initiate goeth through it proudly, like a princess, knowing it but serves to increase her glory.

But this can only be done by the aid of another intelligence and in a circle, to prevent the power thus generated being lost. Priests attempt to do the same with their scourgings and mortifications of the flesh. But lacking the aid of bonds and their attention being distracted by their scourging themselves and what little power they do produce being dissipated, as they do not usually work within a circle, it is little wonder that they oft fail. Monks and hermits do better, as they are apt to work in tiny cells and caves, which in some ways act as circles. The Knights of the Temple, who used mutually to scourge each other in an octagon, did better stil; but they apparently did not know the virtue of bonds and did evil, man to man.

But perhaps some did know. What of the Church's charge that they wore girdles or cords?

To Get the Sight

Sight cometh to different people in divers ways; 'tis seldom it cometh naturally, but it can be induced in many ways. Deep and prolonged meditation may do it, but only if you are a natural, and usually prolonged fasting is necessary. Of old the monks and nuns obtained visions by long vigils, combined with fasting and flagellation til blood came; other mortifications of the flesh were practiced which resulted in visions.

In the East 'tis tried with various tortures whilst sitting in a cramped position, which retarded the flow of blood; these tortures, long and continued, gave good results.

In the Art, we are taught an easier way, that is, to intensify the imagination, at the same time controlling the blood supply, and this may best be done by using the ritual.

Incense is good to propitiate the spirits, also to induce relaxation to the aspirant and to help build up the atmosphere which is necessary for suggestibility. Myrrh, Gum Mastic, Aromatic Rush Roots, Cinnamon Bark, Musk, Juniper, Sandalwood and Ambergris, in combination, are all good, but the best of all is Patchouli.

The circle being formed, and everything properly prepared,

the aspirant should first bind and take his tutor into the circle, invoke suitable spirits for the operation, dance round till giddy, meanwhile invoking and announcing the object of the work, then he should use the flagellum. Then the tutor should in turn bind the aspirant - but very lightly, so as not to cause discomfort - but enough to retard the blood slightly. Again they should dance round, then at the Altar the tutor should use the flagellum with light, steady, slow and monotonous strokes. It is very important that the pupil should see the strokes coming, as this has the effect of passing, and helps greatly to stimulate the imagination. It is important that the strokes be not hard, the object being to do no more than draw the blood to that part and away from the brain; this, with the light binding, slowing down the circulation of the blood, and the passes, soon induce a drowsy stupor. The tutor should watch for this, and as soon as the aspirant speaks or sleeps the flagellum should cease. The tutor should also watch that the pupil becomes not cold, and if the pupil struggles or seems distressed he should at once be awakened.

Be not discouraged if no results come at the first experiment - results usually occur after two or three attempts. It will be found that after two or three attempts or experiments results will come, and soon more quickly; also soon much of the ritual may be shortened, but never forget to invoke the Goddess or to form the circle, and for good results 'tis ever better to do too much ritual rather than do too little at first.

It has been found that this practice doth often cause a fondness between aspirant and tutor, and it is a cause of better results if this be so. If for any reason it is undesireable there be any great fondness between aspirant and tutor this may easily be avoided by both parties from the onset, by firmly resolving in their minds that if any fondness ensues it shall be that of a brother and sister, or parent and child, and it is for this reason that a man may only be taught by a woman and a woman by a man, and that man and man or woman and woman should never attempt these practices together, and may all the curses of the Mighty Ones be on any who make such an attempt. Remember, the circle properly constructed is ever necessary to prevent the power released being dissipated; it is also a barrier against any disturbing or mischievious forces; for to obtain good results you must be free from all disturbances.

Remember, darkness, points of light gleaming amid the surrounding dark, incense and the steady passes by a white arm, are not as stage effects but rather they are mechanical instruments which serve to start the suggestion which later unlocks the knowledge that it is possible to obtain the divine ecstacy, and so attain to knowledge and communication with the Divine Goddess. When once you have attained this, ritual is needless, as you may attain the state of ecstacy at will, but 'til then or, if having obtained or attained it yourself, you wish to bring a companion to that state of joy, ritual is best.

To Leave the Body

'Tis not wise to strive to get out of your body until you have thoroughly gained the Sight. The same ritual as to gain the Sight may be used, but have a comfortable couch. Kneel so that you have your thigh, belly and chest well supported, the arms strained forward and bound one on each side, so that there is a decided feeling of being pulled forward. As the trance is induced, you should feel a striving to push yourself out of the top of your head. The scourge should be given a dragging action, as if to drive or drag you out. Both wills should be thoroughly in tune, keeping a constant and equal strain. When trance comes, your tutor may help you by softly calling your name. You will probably feel yourself drawn out of your body as if through a narrow opening, and find yourself standing beside your tutor, looking at the body on the couch. Strive to communicate with your tutor first; if they have the Sight they will probably see you. Go not far afield at first, and 'tis better to have one who is used to leaving the body with you.

A note: When, having succeeded in leaving the body, you desire to return, in order to cause the spirit body and the material body to coincide, **THINK OF YOUR FEET**. This will cause the return to take place.

The Working Tools

There are no magical supply shops, so unless you are lucky enough to be given or sold tools, a poor witch must extemporise. But when made you should be able to borrow or obtain an Athame. So having made your circle, erect an altar. Any small table or chest will do. There must be fire on it (a candle will suffice) and your book. For good results incense is best if you can get it, but coals in a chafing dish burning sweet-smelling herbs will do. A cup if you would have cakes and wine and a platter with the signs drawn into same in ink, showing a pentacle. A scourge is easily made (note, the scourge has eight tails and five knots in each tail). Get a white-hilted knife and a wand (a sword is not necessary). Cut the marks with Athame. Purify everything, then consecrate your tools in proper form and ever be properly prepared. But ever remember, magical operations are useless unless the mind can be brought to the proper attitude, keyed to the uttmost pitch.

Affirmations must be made clearly and the mind should be inflamed with desire. With this frenzy of will you may do as much with simple tools as with the most complete set. But good and especially ancient tools have their own aura. They do help to bring about that reverential spirit, the desire to learn and develop your powers. For this reason witches ever try to obtain tools from sorcerers, who being skilled men make good tools and consecrate them well, giving them mighty power. But a great witch's tools also gain much power; and you should ever strive to make any tools you manufacture of the finest materials you can obtain, to the end that they may absorb your power the more easily. And of course if you may inherit or obtain another witch's tools, power will flow from them.

Making Tools

It is an old belief that the best substances for making tools are those that once had life in them, as opposed to artificial substances. Thus, wood or ivory is better for a wand than metal, which is more appropriate for swords or knives. Virgin parchment is better than manufactured paper for talismans, etc. And things which have been made by hand are good, because there is life in them.

To Make Anointing Ointment

Take a glazed pan half full of grease or olive oil. Put in sweet mint leaves bruised. Place pan in hot water bath. Stir occasionally. After four or five hours pour into linen bag and squeeze grease through into pot again and fill with fresh leaves. Repeat until grease is strongly scented. Do same with marjoram, thyme and pounded dried patchouli leaves, an you may have them (for they be best of all). When strongly scented, mix all the greases together and keep in a well-stoppered jar.

Anoint behind ears, throat, breasts and womb. In rites where Blessed be ... may be said, anoint knees and feet, as also for rites connected with journeys or war.

Various Instructions

A note upon the ritual of the Wine and Cakes. It is said that in olden days ale or mead was often used instead of wine. It is said that spirits or anything can be used, "so long as it has life" (i.e. has a kick).
All are brothers and sisters, for this reason; that even the High Priestess must submit to the scourge.

The only exception to the rule that a man only be initiated by a woman and a woman by a man, is that a mother may initiate her daughter and a father his son, because they are part of themselves.
A woman may impersonate either the God or the Goddess, but a man may only impersonate the God.

Ever remember, if tempted to admit or boast of belonging to the cult, you may be endangering your brothers and sisters. For though now the fires of persecution have died down, who knows when they may be revived? Many priests have knowledge of our secrets and they full well know that much religious bigotry has died down or calmed down, that many people would wish to join our cult if the truth were known of its joys and the churches would lose power. So if we take many recruits we may loose the fires of persecution against us again. So ever keep the secrets.

Those taking part in a rite must know exactly what results they wish to attain and must keep all their minds firmly fixed on the desired result, without wavering.

The Witches' Round

Nowadays used to raise the Cone of Power, this old dance may be used alone or in full coven. It is better if the Drawing Down of the Moon has gone before, for then the Gods shall fuse with the energies raised in the ecstacy of the dance and thereby accomplish your will.

All join hands to form a ring about the HPS. Heads turned left and eyes tightly shut, will a flowing river of power about the circle, moving from one through the next, from man to woman and woman to man, about the circle without beginning or end, gathering strength as it goes.

When the circle is set thus, in motionless intensity, the HPS begins to clap to the rhythym of the heart-beat. And upon this signal all open their eyes and step widdershins; slowly at first but with a quickening step as the HPS quickens the beat of her clap, until three rounds are complete. And this must be accomplished smoothly and without awkwardness.

Now change direction and dance deosil to the Witches' Rune or some other tune; slowly at first, but faster and ever faster until, the Power being at its peak, the HPS shall release it crying: "Down !", whereupon all shall fall to the ground to sit in a circle facing in. Thus also was the Cone of Power raised of yore.

Bibliography:

These sources have published parts of the text included in this book.

The Witche's Way- Janet and Stewart Ferrar

Eight Sabbats for Witche's- Ferrar

What Witche's Do- Doreen Valiente

Grimoire of Lady Sheba

Birth of Witchcraft- Doreen Valiente

Witchcraft for Tomarrow- Doreen Valiente

GBG- BOS

GBG- High Magick

Alex Sanders BOS

Lady Shebas BOS

Witche's Qabala- Ellen Cannon Reed

Star Hawks Spiral Dance

King of The Witche's- June John

Church of The Seven Arrows

Witche's Almanac- 1971-72

Blessed Be!